CW01267225

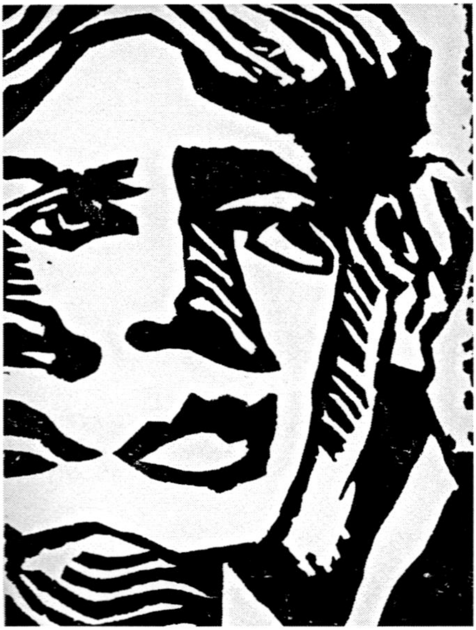

POEMS BY
ESENIN

translated by

CHARLES BRASCH

AND

PETER SOSKICE

WITH ILLUSTRATIONS FROM
WOODCUTS BY WAYNE SEYB

COLD HUB PRESS

© Charles Brasch and Peter Soskice 1970
© The Estate of Charles Brasch 2015

Illustrations © Wayne Seyb 2015

Cold Hub Press
PO Box 156
Lyttelton 8841
New Zealand
coldhubpress.co.nz

ISBN: 978-0-473-31391-3

A catalogue record for this book is available from the National Library of New Zealand.

Poems by Esenin was first published in 1970 by Wai-te-ata Press, Department of English, Victoria University of Wellington.

Many thanks to Alan Roddick, literary executor of the estate of Charles Brasch, for his assistance with, and enthusiasm for, this project.

Contents

 7 About the translations

 9 *Look, evening now (1910)*
10 *Beggars wandered through villages (1910)*
11 *Dark night, I cannot sleep (1911)*
12 *A white birch tree (1913)*
13 *Good Morning (1914)*
14 *Beloved country, my heart dreams (1914)*
15 *You my neglected country (1914)*
16 *First Snow ((1914)*
17 *Beyond the darkly woven thicket (1915-16)*
18 *Here with my own people (1915-16)*
19 *Dawn is a red fence (1917)*
20 *O fields, fields, fields (1917-18)*
21 *There must be happiness (1917-18)*
22 *Confession of a Hooligan (1920)*
25 *Evening has knitted its dark brows (1923)*
26 *Another may have drunk your love (1923)*
28 *Gazing at you makes me sad (1923)*
29 *Letter to his Mother (1924)*
31 *Snowstorm (1924)*
35 *To Kachalov's Dog (1925)*
36 *The flowers are saying goodbye (1925)*
37 *Cold gold of the moon (1925)*
38 *Recollection (1925)*
39 *What a night! I lie helpless (1925)*

41 Notes to the poems

About the Translations

Sergei Esenin (the name is pronounced Yesenin, stress on the second syllable) is one of the most widely read and loved of all Russian poets. The great fame he won in his short life has hardly dimmed since. He was born in 1895 of a peasant family in the village of Konstantinovo, Ryazan Province, Central Russia, and died by his own hand in Leningrad on 28 December 1925.

He was a prolific writer. Although the poems translated here represent only a fraction of his work, they include versions of some of his best poems, and in their variety may suggest his range. We have tried to catch in English something of Esenin's directness and vitality, and to render as literally as possible what often seems the extreme verbal shorthand of his rich and arresting imagery. In poems in regular stanza form we have aimed at the rhythm of the Russian, which meant sacrificing rhyme; but it is worth noting that Esenin and other Russian poets constantly use, among their perfect rhymes, ones corresponding to the English love-move, coming-running, upon-Goneril, and the like. The poems are dated, and printed in chronological order.

P.S. 1970

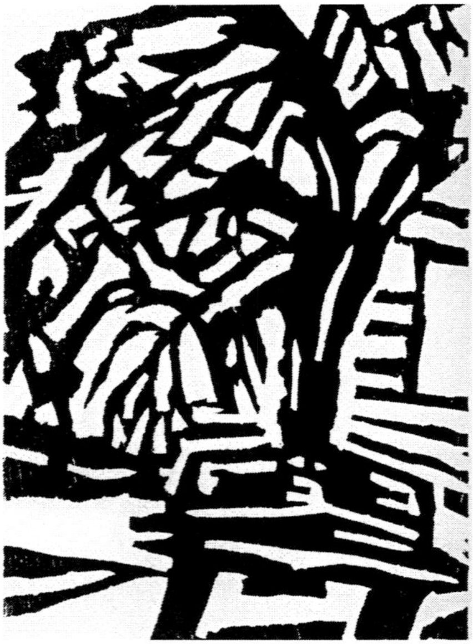

Look, evening now

Look, evening now. The dew
Is glistening on a nettle.
I stand beside the road
My back against a willow.

Broad moonlight falls
Straight on our cottage roof.
Somewhere far off I hear
The song of a nightingale.

It's pleasant here and warm
As in winter by the stove.
And the birches, silver,
Stand like great candles.

And far beyond the river,
Beyond the forest border,
Goes the drowsy watchman
Beating his wooden clapper.

Beggars wandered through villages

Beggars wandered through villages,
Under the windows drank kvas,
Before the locked doors of old churches
Bowed down to the Holy Saviour.

Strangers, they wandered through fields,
Chanting verses about the sweet Jesus.
Past laden beasts plodded on
As cackling geese joined in their song.

They limped through the herds wretchedly
Telling long sufferings over:
"One God only we serve,
Lay penance of chains on our shoulders."

Quickly they took from their wallets
Scraps they had saved up for cows.
And shepherd girls mockingly shouted:
"The holy buffoons are here! Dance!"

Dark night, I cannot sleep

Dark night, I cannot sleep,
But walk to the river meadow.
Summer lightning breaks loose
To plunge in the foaming waters.

On the hillock a birch-tree candle
Silvered by the moon's feathers.
Come out, my heart, and listen
To the psaltery-player's song.

Shall I gaze wonderingly
Lost in your girlish beauty?
No, I'll dance to the strings,
Tearing the veil from your face.

To the dark room, to the green wood,
To the silken river reeds,
I'll carry you off past the hills
Right to poppy dawn.

A white birch tree

A white birch tree
Underneath my window
Has clad itself in snow
As though all in silver.

On the furry branches
With their edge of snow
Fingers have opened out
And made a white fringe.

And the birch tree stands
In a sleepy silence,
And snowflakes blaze
In golden fire.

While the dawn, lazily
Spreading on every side,
Again upon the branches
Hangs new silver.

Good Morning

Gold stars begin to drowse,
The mirror of the creek trembles,
Light dawns on dull backwaters
And reddens the gauze sky.

Sleepy birches smile,
Ruffling their silken tresses.
Green catkins rustle
And dewdrops shine silver.

By the fence, a shaggy nettle
Hung with bright mother-of-pearl
Swaying whispers playfully:
"Good morning".

Beloved country, my heart dreams

Beloved country! My heart dreams of
Haystack suns in clear waters.
Would I could lose myself among
The hundred voices of your greenness.

See, to mark the boundary-strip,
Mignonette and clover chalice.
And whispering to their rosaries
Stand the gentle willow nuns.

The marsh smoke turns to cloud,
Burning in the yoke of heaven.
With quiet secrecy I hold
Thoughts for someone in my heart.

All things I greet, accept all,
Gladly lay my soul bare.
I have come to this earth
So that I may leave it sooner.

You my neglected country

You my neglected country, you
My country, a wilderness
Of grass uncut at harvest-time,
Of forest and monastery.

Old huts are leaning there together,
Five of them in all.
Their roofs begin to foam into
The log path of dawn.

Under a straw chasuble
Rotted rafter wood,
Wind sprinkles sunlight over
The dove-coloured mould.

Ravens beat unceasingly
Wings on window-panes,
The bird-cherry tree like a snowstorm
Is tossing up its sleeve.

Is not your past and present life
A tale told in the bushes,
That once the steppe-grass whispered to
A traveller at dusk?

First Snow

I ride in silence. On the snow
I hear the sound of horses' hooves.
Only the grey crows
Noisily disturb the meadow.

Spellbound by an unseen spirit
The forest is dreaming a fairy-tale,
As if a white kerchief had
Been tied about a pine-tree's hair.

It bends down, like an old woman
Leaning on her crutch;
At its very top, a woodpecker
Is chiselling on a bough.

My horse bounds over wide spaces.
The snow drifts high, spreading a shawl.
The ribbon of the endless highway
Runs on and on into the distance.

Beyond the darkly woven thicket

Beyond the darkly woven thicket
In deep blue untroubled air
A curly lambkin moon is out
Playing on the dove-blue grass.

Its horns seem to butt against
The sedges of the lulled lake
And even against distant paths,
Making the waters rock the shore.

Under the steppe's green coverlet
The bird-cherries smoke with incense,
And on slopes beyond the valleys
Flame wavers overhead.

O land of feather-grass, deep forest,
Close to my steady-beating heart,
Even in your depth is hidden
The melancholy of the salt-marsh.

You too in cruel sacrifice
Confusing friend and enemy
Grieve for rosy heavens again
And the pigeon-winging clouds.

But from the blue steppe-land spaces
Darkness, with a timid finger,
Points to your Siberian fetters
And the humpbacked Ural range.

Here with my own people

Here with my own people again,
My country, I am pensive, tender.
Curling dusk beyond the hill
Waves a hand of snowy whiteness.

The grey hairs of a gloomy day
Are drifting past, unkempt, dishevelled,
And evening sadness troubles me
So deeply I am left defenceless.

Over the church dome since dawn
A shadow has been sinking lower.
O friends of my old games and pleasures,
I have seen you for the last time.

The years have vanished without trace,
And you went after them somewhere.
Only the same noisy water
Beyond the winged mill keeps on running.

And often in the evening haze,
Hearing the sound of trampled sedge,
I implore the smoking earth
For things far gone beyond recall.

Dawn is a red fence

Dawn is a red fence over the field.
On a cloudlet floats the Eternal Son.

Granny comes out to feed her chicks.
The Holy Image burns in the sky.

— Hullo, grandson!
                — Hullo, old dear!
— Come into the hut.
                — Is grandad there?

— He's mending the net to catch us some fish.
— Has grandad many years in his dish?

— He'll soon knock ninety winters back. —
And grandson flies up like white smoke.

With grandad's soul he sails to the clouds,
Where noon looks down on invisible lands.

O fields, fields, fields

O fields, fields, fields,
The sadness of Kolomna;
Heavy the past on my heart,
But in my heart shines Russia.

Like birds, the milestones whistle
From under my horse's hooves,
And the sun sprinkles me
With handfuls of his rain.

O land of threatening flood
And of spring's quiet power,
Here by dawn and stars
I took my way to school.

Pondering, I read
The bible of the winds,
And Isaiah with me
Pastured my golden cows.

There must be happiness

There must be happiness, I know it!
The sun itself has not gone out.
Dawn with its red prayer-book is here
Prophesying glad news to come.
There must be happiness, I know it!

Ring out, ring out, O golden Russia,
Rise indefatigable wind!
Blessed the man who notes with joy
The shepherd sadness of your land.
Ring out, ring out, O golden Russia!

I love the murmur of wild waters
And stars shining on the wave.
Blessed be your suffering,
Let my people give its blessing.
I love the murmur of wild waters.

Confession of a Hooligan

Not every man can sing,
Not every man is free to fall
Like an apple, at other men's feet.

This is the greatest confession
A hooligan ever confessed.

On purpose I walk about unkempt,
Head like a kerosene lamp on my shoulders.
I like to light up in the dark
The leafless autumn of your souls.
I like it when stones of abuse
Fly at me like hail of belching storms.
I simply press my hands more firmly
On the reeling bubble of my hair.

How gladly I remember then
The overgrown pond and the creaking of the alder;
That somewhere my father and mother are living,
Who do not care a pin for all my poems,
Though I am dear to them as field and flesh
And the small rain that stirs the green in spring.
They would come stabbing at you with pitchforks
For every shout you hurled at me.

Poor poor peasants!
You must be ugly now,
Still as fearful of God and of marshy depths.
O, if only you would understand
That your son is the best
Poet in Russia!

Did not your hearts turn cold with fear for his life
When he dipped bare feet in autumn puddles?
And now he goes in a top hat
And patent-leather shoes.

But underneath he is still the lively
Mischievous village boy.
He bows from a distance
To every cow on the sign of a butcher's shop.
And meeting the cabmen in the square,
Remembering the smell of dung from his father's fields,
He is ready to carry every horse's tail
Like the train of a bridal gown.

I love my native land.
Dearly I love my native land!
Though on it lies the osier rust of grief.
I like the dirtied snouts of pigs
And in night stillness the ringing voice of toads.
I am tender-sick with memory of childhood,
I dream of the dew and damp of April evenings.
Our maple tree seemed to squat down as if
To warm itself at the bonfire of dawn.
O, how many times clambering up its branches
I stole eggs from the ravens' nests!
Is it the same tree still, with top of green,
And the strong bark it had?

And you, my darling,
Faithful piebald dog?
Whining and blind with old age
You prowl about the yard, dragging your flabby tail,
Your scent for door and cowshed lost.

How dear to me are all your tricks;
When I had stolen a hunk of bread from mother
We would share it bite for bite,
Not robbing each other of a crumb.

I am just the same still.
At heart I am just the same still.
Like cornflowers in the rye my eyes flower in my face.
Spreading the gilded mats of poems,
I want to say tender words to you.

Good night!
To all of you, good night!
Over the twilight grass the scythe of dawn has stopped ringing . . .
I long tonight
For the moon outside my window . . .

Blue light, light so blue!
In that blue even to die would be no grief.
Well, what if I do seem a cynic
With a lamp hitched to his backside!
My good old hard-worked Pegasus,
Do I not still need your gentle trot?
I came like a severe master
To sing and glorify the rats.
My head is like August,
My hair flows like seething wine.

I want to be the yellow sail
Bound for that land we are sailing to.

Evening has knitted its dark brows

Evening has knitted its dark brows.
Someone's horses are standing in the yard.
Wasn't it yesterday I drank away my youth?
Didn't I stop loving you yesterday?

No panting, troika, although you're late.
Our life has swept past without a trace.
Tomorrow perhaps a hospital bed
Will take me in to rest forever.

Tomorrow perhaps I shall go away
A different being, healed for good,
To listen to the songs of showers and bird-cherry
Trees for which a sound man lives.

I shall forget the gloomy powers
Tormenting and destroying me.
O tender face, beloved face,
You alone I shall not forget.

Suppose I come to love another,
I must tell her then, that other,
Tell her of you I used to love,
You whom once I called my love.

I shall tell her how our past
Life slipped by, but was not past . . .
O my mind, you so daring,
What have you brought me to at last?

Another may have drunk your love

Another may have drunk your love,
But these remain for me no less,
The glassy smoke that is your hair
And your eyes' autumn weariness.

O age of autumn! To me now
Dearer even than youth and summer.
Doubly you have come to please
The imagination of a poet.

In my heart I never lie,
So to that swaggerer's voice of mine
Unhesitating I can say
I shall cut out the hooligan.

Time to be done with pranks and brawls,
The unruliness on which I fed.
Another brew has slaked my heart,
One that sobers up the blood.

September at my window knocks
With a crimson branch of willow,
Telling me to be ready and
Meet soberly its sober coming.

I am reconciled to many things,
Without loss, without constraint.
Russia seems different to me,
Its huts and cemeteries different.

With clear gaze I look around
And here, there, anywhere I see
That only you, sister and friend,
Could keep a poet company.

That to you alone I could,
Being brought up in constancy,
Sing about the dusk roads,
And one who is done with hooliganry.

Gazing at you makes me sad

Gazing at you makes me sad,
Such pain I feel, such pity too,
Knowing that we are left in September
Only with the bronze willow.

Others' lips have kissed away
Your warm and palpitating body,
As if a small rain were drizzling
From a soul part numb already.

Well, I have no fear of that.
What I feel is a different joy.
Nothing, you see, is left me now
But yellow dampness and decay.

I have not spared myself, you see,
For a quiet life, for smiling faces.
So few the roads that I have travelled,
So many blunders I have made.

Ludicrous my disordered life,
So it was and so will be,
A garden like a graveyard, strewed
With the gnawed bones of birch trees.

So we too shall fade, and fall
Silent, like the garden's guests.
If there are no flowers in winter
Then we need not mourn for them.

Letter to his Mother

Are you alive still, old and dear one?
I am alive too. Greetings, greetings!
May that ineffable evening light
Still fall streaming on your hut.

They tell me you are anxious for me,
Saddened to learn about my life,
That you often walk the road
Wearing an ancient threadbare cloak.

And that in the blue evening dusk
One scene often comes to you:
A bar-room brawl, and someone sticking
A Finnish dagger in my ribs.

No, dear, set your mind at rest.
That's harmful fancy, nothing more.
I'm not yet such a bitter drunkard
That I could die without seeing you.

I am as loving as before
And dream always of one thing only,
This restless anguish shaken off
To come back soon to our small house.

I shall come back when our white orchard
Spreads its branches for the spring.
But then, don't wake me up at dawn
As you did eight years ago.

Do not wake burned-out dreams,
Do not stir up what could not be —
Too early in my life I learned
To suffer loss and weariness.

And do not teach me to pray. Not that!
There's no returning to the past.
You alone are my help and comfort,
You alone my ineffable light.

So, then, forget your anxious fear,
Do not be sad about my life.
And do not walk the road so often
Wearing your ancient threadbare cloak.

Snowstorm

Spin, days, your thread of old,
A living soul can never be remade.
No!
I shall never get on with myself,
To my darling self
I am a stranger.

I want to read, but the book slips from my hand,
I am overcome with yawning,
And almost asleep . . .
And outside the window
Long drawn out the wind sobbing
As if it felt
The nearness of death.

A tattered maple tree
Black at the top
Hoarsely and nasally drones
Past history to the sky.
What kind of maple is it?
Just a shameful post
To hang a man on
Or to be cut down for scrap.

And first
They'd better hang me,
Crossing my hands behind my back —
Because with song
Hoarse and sickly
I kept from sleep
My native land.

I have no love for
The song of the cock long drawn-out
And I declare
That if I had the power
I would tear out the entrails
Of all cocks
So that they couldn't
Give voice by night.

But I forget
I am a cock myself
Shouting aloud
Before daybreak on earth,
Trampling my father's precepts,
Troubled at heart
And in my verse.

The storm is shrieking
Like a wild boar
They have come to kill.
Cold
Icy mist,
You can't make out
What's far off,
What's near . . .

The moon, most likely,
Has been eaten by the dogs —
For a long time
It hasn't been seen in the sky.
Drawing out a flax thread
From the spindle
My mother keeps on talking.

The deaf cat
Listens to her talk,
Hanging from the stove ledge
His heavy head.
Not for nothing
Scared neighbours say
That he is like
A black owl.

My eyes close,
And as I screw them tight
I see a vision
From fairy-tale times:
The cat with one paw
Shows me the fig,
And my mother is like a witch
From Kiev mountain.

I do not know whether
I am ill or not ill,
But my thoughts
Wander in disorder.
In my ears is the sepulchral
Knock of spades
With the distant sobbing
Of church bells.

I see myself
Dead in the grave
Under the moaning
Alleluias of the priest.
I draw down lower
My own dead eyelids,

Placing on them
Two copper pieces.

This money
From dead eyes
Will warm the grave-digger's heart —
Having buried me
At once he will take
A glass of raw brandy.

And he will say loudly,
"There's a queer fish!
He lived it up all right
In his life . . .
Yet he couldn't get through
Even five pages
Of *Capital*."

To Kachalov's Dog

Give me your paw, Jim, do, just for luck.
I've never seen a paw like that in my life.
Let us bark together by moonlight
In the stillness, when there's no sound to be heard.
Give me your paw, Jim, do, just for luck.

Please, old fellow, don't go licking me.
We'll hunt together, just we two.
You haven't a notion what life means,
You don't know what it takes to live on earth.

He's a kind man, your master, and well-known,
And his house is always full of visitors,
And every one, smiling, looks for a chance
To touch and stroke your velvet fur.

You're devilish handsome in your dog's way
With that charming trustful friendliness of yours.
And, not begging a crumb from anybody,
Like a drunk friend, you nose up for a kiss.

Dear Jim, among your many visitors
Were ones of every kind and of no kind.
But she, most sad and quiet of them all,
Did she drop in here suddenly by chance?

She'll come again, I swear to you she will,
And if I am not there, fix your eyes on her,
Lick her hand tenderly for me,
For all my guilt and all my innocence.

The flowers are saying goodbye

The flowers are saying goodbye to me,
Drooping their heads, down, down,
Because I shall not see her face
Again, nor see my native land.

Well, darling, if it must be — well!
I have seen them all and seen the earth,
And I shall take this coffin-trembling
As if it were a new caress.

Because I have understood it all,
This life, and passed by smilingly,
I can say again each moment
That everything on earth returns.

What matter — someone else will come,
No grief consume the man that's gone,
Will come to make a better song
For my dear deserted one.

And listening to that song in stillness,
You, dear, with another love,
May remember me perhaps,
A flower that will not return.

Cold gold of the moon

Cold gold of the moon,
Scent of oleander and stock.
How good it is to roam the peace
Of this blue caressing land.

There's Bagdad, far and farther off,
Where Sheherazade lived and sang.
Now she has need of nothing. The sounds
Of the garden ceased sounding long ago.

Churchyard grass has overgrown
The distant ghosts of earth.
Pay no heed to the dead, traveller,
Nor bow your head to their tombstones.

Look, how lovely all things here:
Your lips long and long for roses.
Only forgive your enemy at heart
And saffron bliss will breathe on you.

You would live? then live; love? fall in love.
In moonlight gold walk and kiss.
If you must bow before the dead
Don't poison the living with your dreams.

Even Sheherazade sang it,
As the bronze of leaves tells again.
To those who have need of nothing, we
Can only offer pity on earth.

Recollection

October now is not the same.
It's not the same October now.
In this land, where foul weather whistles,
October raged and howled
Like a wild beast,
October 1917.
I remember the terrible
Snowy day.
I saw with dulled eyes.
An iron shadow hung
Over darkened Petrograd.
Now everyone smelt the coming storm,
Now everyone knew it,
Knew.
Not for nothing soldiers carried
Tortoises of steel.
They scattered . . .
They formed up in ranks . . .
The people tremble in fear . . .
And someone suddenly tears a placard
From the wall of a timid concierge.
And it has started . . .
Eyes darted round
Burning with civil war,
And from the smoke of a fiery 'Aurora'
An iron dawn has risen.
The fatal lot is cast,
And over the land at the cry of "Bugger off",
A fiery sign has shot up:
'The Soviet of the Workers' Deputies.'

What a night! I lie helpless

What a night! I lie helpless —
How can I ever sleep. Such moonlight!
It seems as if in soul I stand
On guard over my lost youth.

Friend of years grown cold now,
Do not call our love a game,
No, but let this moonlight shed
Its slanting rays onto my pillow.

Let it light up boldly my
Distorted features — you see now
You cannot simply cease to love
Who never learned to love at all.

We can love once and only once.
You are a stranger to me because
The lime-trees beckon us in vain,
Plunging their feet in drifts of snow.

I know well, as you also know,
That in this moonlight, gleaming blue,
There are no blossoms on these limes,
But only hoarfrost over snow.

That we have long fallen out of love —
Each of us loves another now,
And both of us indifferently
Can play the worthless game of love.

Yet fondle and enfold me still
In the cunning passion of a kiss,
Let me eternally dream of May
And one whom I shall love for ever.

NOTES TO THE POEMS

Look, evening now: The reference is to the *kolotushka*, a sort of wooden rattle or clapper, by means of which the night watchman announced his presence and assured the sleeping village that all was well.

Confession of a Hooligan: The word *khuligan* (hooligan) appears often in Esenin's later poems, where it means a dissipated and disorderly style of living, and not rowdyism as such, although it includes an element of drunken brawling and destructiveness.

Cold gold of the moon: This and other poems not here printed, *My former pain is laid to rest* and *I have never been on the Bosphorus*, belong to the 'Persian Cycle' of fifteen poems in a would-be oriental manner, rich in imagery and hyperbole, which Esenin wrote in the Caucasus in 1924 and 1925. They show the great attraction which Persia had for him; he always hoped to go there, but never did so.

Recollection: The 'Aurora' was the battleship whose guns fired on the Winter Palace, so beginning the revolution.